NFL TEAM STORIES

The Story of the
MINNESOTA VIKINGS

By Craig Ellenport

Kaleidoscope
Minneapolis, MN

The Quest for Discovery Never Ends

• •

This edition first published in 2021 by Kaleidoscope Publishing, Inc.

No part of this publication may be reproduced in whole or in part without written permission of the publisher.

For information regarding permission, write to
Kaleidoscope Publishing, Inc.
6012 Blue Circle Drive
Minnetonka, MN 55343

Library of Congress Control Number
2020936024

ISBN
978-1-64519-237-4 (library bound)
978-1-64519-305-0 (ebook)

Text copyright © 2021 by Kaleidoscope Publishing, Inc. All-Star Sports, Bigfoot Books, and associated logos are trademarks and/or registered trademarks of Kaleidoscope Publishing, Inc.

Printed in the United States of America.

FIND ME IF YOU CAN!

Bigfoot lurks within one of the images in this book. It's up to you to find him!

TABLE OF CONTENTS

Kickoff! 4

Chapter 1: Vikings History 6

Chapter 2: Vikings All-Time Greats 16

Chapter 3: Vikings Superstars 22

Beyond the Book 28
Research Ninja 29
Further Resources 30
Glossary 31
Index 32
Photo Credits 32
About the Author 32

KICKOFF!

AAAH-OOOOHH-AAH!

That's the sound of a huge horn. The instrument is called a gjallarhorn [YAL-er-horn]. The sound blasts across U.S. Bank Stadium! A Minnesota Vikings game is about to start. Fans cheer!

A Vikings hero blows the horn before each game.

The Vikings take their name from long-ago people. In a Viking legend, Heimdall guarded the gates to the gods' home. He blew the gjallarhorn. That signalled the gods for a battle. Now the horn sounds for the Minnesota Vikings. A different Vikings hero gets the honor each game. When the giant horn blasts, it's time for kickoff! Let's find out more about this great NFL team.

Chapter 1
Vikings History

The Vikings played their first 21 seasons outdoors in the cold!

The state of Minnesota used to have two NFL teams. The Minneapolis Marines (also called the Red Jackets) played from 1921 to 1930. The Duluth Eskimos were on the field from 1923 to 1927. After those teams folded, pro football left Minnesota for a long time.

In 1961, the Minnesota Vikings joined the NFL. The team's name comes from the state's **Nordic** roots. The Vikings put on the purple and gold for the first time against the Chicago Bears. The Vikings won their first game ever!

FUN FACT
The Vikings' first coach was Hall of Fame QB Norm Van Brocklin.

Duluth was home to an NFL team in the 1920s. The Eskimos wore an igloo on the front of their jerseys!

Joe Kapp led the Vikings to Super Bowl IV.

The Vikings' early seasons were not that good. The team got better quickly. They won the National Football Conference (NFC) in 1969. That put them into Super Bowl IV. Minnesota lost there to Kansas City 23–7. But it was the start of a great decade for the Vikings.

In the 1970s, the team played in three more Super Bowls. In 1973 and 1974, they even went back-to-back! Unfortunately, they lost all three games. Still, Vikings fans watched a lot of great players. The team was led by its great **defensive line**. They were called the Purple People Eaters. The name came from a popular song title.

Alan Page

Jim Marshall

Gary Larsen

Carl Eller

In the 1980s, wide receiver Cris Carter was the team's star. He helped Minnesota reach the playoffs five times. The Vikings won the NFC Central **Division** twice. The NFL had six divisions in those days. The league has eight now. Today's Vikings play in the NFC North.

The 1990s were great for the Vikings. They reached the playoffs seven times. They never had a

MEET THE MASCOT

Viktor the Viking helps Vikings fans cheer. A huge helmet covers his bright blond hair. The team says that Viktor is a real Viking. He was frozen in Lake Superior until 2007. Then he came out to root for the team. The Vikings used to have a human mascot called Ragnar.

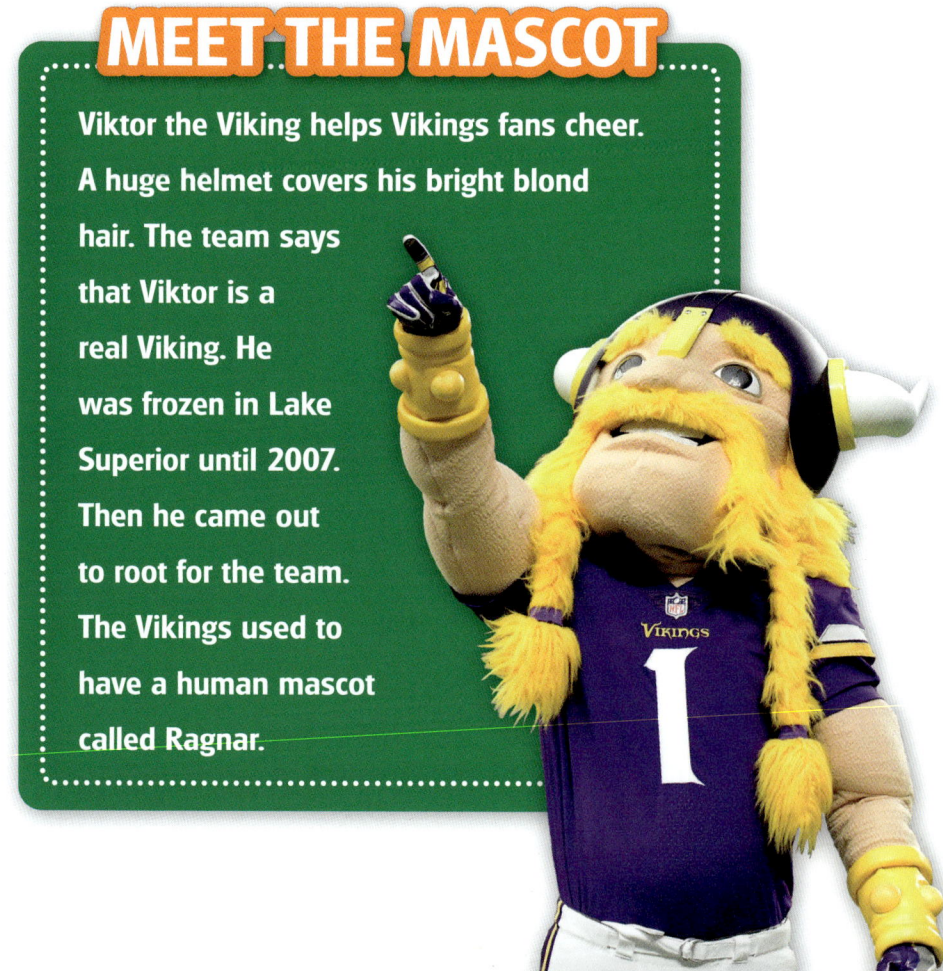

losing record from 1991 to 2000. In 1998, they played in the NFC Championship Game. (See page 14.)

The Vikings struggled in the early 2000s. They were never really bad. But they were not that good, either! In 2009, they put it all together. Superstar Brett Favre took over at QB. He led the team to the NFC Championship Game. New Orleans needed **overtime** to knock out the Vikings.

Brett Favre aims for the end zone!

In 2017, the Vikings won the NFC North Division. It was their second division title in three years. In January 2018, the Vikings pulled off the Minneapolis Miracle. The team trailed the New Orleans Saints late in the game. On the final play, Kirk Cousins hit Stefon Diggs with a 61-yard TD pass. The Vikings won!

They advanced to the NFC Championship Game. The Vikings scored first. Kyle Rudolph caught a 25-yard pass. That was it, though. The Philadelphia Eagles didn't let Minnesota score again. The Eagles won 38–7!

The Vikings made the playoffs again in 2019. They lost to San Francisco in the second round.

FUN FACT
Diggs led the Vikings with 102 catches in 2018.

TIMELINE OF THE MINNESOTA VIKINGS

1961
1961: Minnesota plays its first NFL game.

1968
1968: Vikings win their first Central Division championship.

1974
1974: Vikings win their second NFC title in a row. They also lose their second Super Bowl in a row!

1976
1976: Minnesota wins the NFC. It loses Super Bowl XI to Oakland.

1998
1998: Vikings set a team record with 15 wins.

2017
2017: The Vikings win 13 games. That is their most since 1998.

2019
2019: Vikings upset the Saints in the Wild Card Playoff Game.

13

WHAT A YEAR!

Vikings fans remember 1998 for good and bad reasons. One good part was the team's 15 wins. Other good parts included watching QB Randall Cunningham and WR Randy Moss. Cunningham threw 34 TD passes. Seventeen of them went to Moss, a new Vikings record.

The Vikings beat the Arizona Cardinals in the first round of the playoffs.

Anderson had not missed a field goal all season. He had made 39 kicks in a row. His first miss came at the worst time!

In the NFC Championship Game against Atlanta, things didn't go as well. The Vikings led 27–20 late in the fourth quarter. Kicker Gary Anderson lined up for a 38-yard field goal. If he made it, Minnesota would surely go to the Super Bowl. He missed!

The Falcons tied the game soon after. In overtime, Atlanta won. Vikings fans were crushed!

Randy Moss made a fingertip grab.

Chapter 2
Vikings All-Time Greats

QB Fran Tarkenton helped the Vikings win the first game in their history. "Fran the Man" **scrambled** to escape tacklers. He couldn't lead the team to the playoffs, however. After playing for the Giants for four seasons, he returned to Minnesota in 1972. In the next five seasons, he led the Vikes to three Super Bowls! Tarkenton has most of the team's all-time passing records.

The Vikings got a new coach in 1967. Bud Grant really turned the team around. He called the shots for all four of the Vikings Super Bowl games.

Fran Tarkenton with Bud Grant

FUN FACT

Tarkenton was the 1975 NFL Most Valuable Player.

FUN FACT
After football, Alan Page became a judge in Minnesota.

Those Super Bowl teams were led by a great defense. The Vikings front four included two future Hall of Famers. Alan Page was a fast defensive tackle. In 1971, he was the NFL MVP. Carl Eller played defensive end. He used his long arms to swarm past blockers. The other starters were end Jim Marshall and tackle Gary Larsen. Marshall played in a team-record 270 games in a row.

Defensive back Paul Krause played behind those guys. Krause had 81 career **interceptions**. That's the most in NFL history.

Krause scored three touchdowns returning interceptions.

In a 1964 game, Jim Marshall picked up this **fumble**. Then he ran the wrong way! He is famous for this mistake.

In the 1990s and early 2000s, Minnesota had stars on offense. Cris Carter and Randy Moss were two of the best receivers of all time. Carter led the NFL in TD catches three times. His 122 catches in 1994 were an NFL record. Several players have broken it since. Moss also led the league in TD catches three times with the Vikings. He used his great height to leap above defenders.

On defense, John Randle led the way. He was fierce and unstoppable. Randle is the Vikings' all-time leader in sacks.

Adrian Peterson played ten seasons for the Vikings through 2016. He led the NFL in rushing three times. He also led in rushing TDs twice. Peterson combined great speed with strength and power. He ran for more yards than any player in Vikings history.

Cris Carter

FUN FACT
Carter was named to eight Pro Bowls, the NFL's all-star game.

VIKINGS
RECORDS

These players piled up the best stats in Vikings history. The numbers are career records through the 2019 season.

Total TDs: Cris Carter, 110

TD Passes: Fran Tarkenton, 239

Passing Yards: Fran Tarkenton, 33,098

Rushing Yards: Adrian Peterson, 11,747

Receptions: Cris Carter, 1,004

Points: Fred Cox, 1,365

Sacks: John Randle, 114

John Randle

Chapter 3
Vikings Superstars

Today's Vikings carry on the great traditions of the team's superstars. QB Kirk Cousins doesn't scramble like Tarkenton. Instead, he has a powerful throwing arm. Cousins plays tough. He has led the team to many big **comeback** wins.

Running back Dalvin Cook is the team's young star. In 2019, he played his third season with the Vikings. It was his best yet. He set a career high with 13 rushing touchdowns. He carried the **rock** 250 times, too.

Minnesota chose Cook in the second round of the 2017 NFL Draft.

Cousins has been the starter since 2018.

Cousins has some great targets for his passes. Stefon Diggs uses his great speed to zoom past defenders. He set a career high with 1,130 receiving yards in 2019. Adam Thielen is another top pass-catcher. Thielen was not drafted by any team after college. He had to earn a spot on the team at a tryout. The Vikings made a good choice! Thielen has 24 TD catches in four years as a starter.

Thielen beats a Giants defender for a TD!

Rudolph makes a key catch against the Lions.

Kyle Rudolph has been the Vikings tight end for nine seasons. He has come through with a lot of big catches for the team.

25

The biggest star on defense is linebacker Anthony Barr. He has been named to four Pro Bowls. The Pro Bowl is the NFL's all-star game. He had a chance to leave Minnesota after 2018. Instead, Barr said that he loved the Vikings. He signed up for another five seasons! Another linebacker star is Eric Kendricks. His main job is stopping running backs. Kendricks led the team in tackles in 2019.

Barr buries a Dolphin!

Smith races home with an interception.

In the secondary, safety Harrison Smith leads the way. Smith has started nearly every Vikings game since 2012.

Can all these players return the Vikings to the top? The team has come very close before. A Super Bowl victory is the next mountain to climb. Then the gjallarhorn can sound again!

BEYOND
THE BOOK

After reading the book, it's time to think about what you learned. Try the following exercises to jumpstart your ideas.

RESEARCH

FIND OUT MORE. Where would you go to find out more about your favorite NFL teams and players? Check out NFL.com, of course. Each team also has its own website. What other sports information sites can you find? See if you can find other cool facts about your favorite team.

CREATE

GET ARTISTIC. Each NFL team has a logo. The Vikings logo shows a mighty Viking horn. Get some art materials and try designing your own Vikings logo. Or create a new team and make a logo for it. What colors would you choose? How would you draw the mascot?

DISCOVER

GO DEEP! As this book shows, the Vikings are still looking for their first Super Bowl win. How do you think each year's team approaches that goal? Do they worry about the past? Or do they focus on the present? How do you think Vikings fans keep cheering no matter what?

GROW

GET OUT AND PLAY! You don't need to be in the NFL to enjoy football. You just need a football and some friends. Play touch or tag football. Or you can hang cloth flags from your belt; grab the belt and make the "tackle." See who has the best arm to be quarterback. Who is the best receiver? Who can run the fastest? Time to play football!

RESEARCH NINJA

Visit **www.ninjaresearcher.com/2374** to learn how to take your research skills and book report writing to the next level!

RESEARCH

DIGITAL LITERACY TOOLS

SEARCH LIKE A PRO
Learn about how to use search engines to find useful websites.

FACT OR FAKE?
Discover how you can tell a trusted website from an untrustworthy resource.

TEXT DETECTIVE
Explore how to zero in on the information you need most.

SHOW YOUR WORK
Research responsibly—learn how to cite sources.

WRITE

GET TO THE POINT
Learn how to express your main ideas.

PLAN OF ATTACK
Learn prewriting exercises and create an outline.

DOWNLOADABLE REPORT FORMS

Further Resources

BOOKS

Olson, Doug. *Stefon Diggs: The Maker of Football Miracles*. Minneapolis: Lake 7 Creative, 2019.

Ryan, Todd. *Minnesota Vikings: Inside the NFL*. Minneapolis: North Star Editions, 2019.

Whiting, Jim. *Minnesota Vikings: NFL Today*. Minneapolis: Creative Paperbacks, 2018.

WEBSITES

FACTSURFER

Factsurfer.com gives you a safe, fun way to find more information.

1. Go to www.factsurfer.com.
2. Enter "Minnesota Vikings" into the search box and click 🔍
3. Select your book cover to see a list of related websites.

Glossary

comeback: When a team rallies from behind to win. The Vikings were behind by 10 points before their comeback.

defensive line: The group of players closest to the football on defense. The defensive line has the first chance to stop running backs.

division: Name for the groups of teams that make up the NFL. The Vikings play in the NFC North Division.

fumble: A ball dropped by a ballcarrier that can be recovered by either team. Dalvin Cook fumbled the ball before he was tackled.

interception: A pass caught by the defense. Harrison Smith made a big interception of a pass by the Packers.

Nordic: Having to do with Norway. Vikings are part of Nordic history.

overtime: The period of play after the fourth quarter ends in a tie. After tying the Lions, the Vikings won in overtime.

rock: A nickname for the football. Cousins dove over the goal line with the rock.

scramble: When a quarterback runs away from the defense. Tarkenton was hard to catch when he scrambled.

Index

Anderson, Gary, 15
Barr, Anthony, 26
Carter, Cris, 10, 20
Cook, Dalvin, 22
Cousins, Kirk, 12, 22, 24
Cunningham, Randall, 14
Diggs, Stefon, 12, 24
Duluth Eskimos, 6
Eller, Carl, 18
Favre, Brett, 11
gjallarhorn, 4, 5, 27
Grant, Bud, 16
Kendricks, Eric, 26

Krause, Paul, 18
Larsen, Gary, 18
Marshall, Jim, 18
Minneapolis Marines, 6
Moss, Randy, 14, 20
Page, Alan, 18
Peterson, Adrian, 20
Purple People Eaters, 9
Randle, John, 20
Rudolph, Kyle, 12
Smith, Harrison, 27
Tarkenton, Fran, 16, 22
Thielen, Adam, 24

PHOTO CREDITS

The images in this book are reproduced through the courtesy of: AP Images: Scott Boehm 4, 6T; 5; 6 Main; Tony Tomsic 8; NFL Photos 9; Ed Reinke 14, 15B; Tom Olmscheid 15, 20; Fred Kaufman 16; PFHOF 19; SF Examiner 19B; Al Messerschmidt 21; Howard Simmons 27. Focus on Football: 17, 18. Newscom: Nick Wosicka/Icon SW 10, 12, 22; Icon SMI 11; Scott Winters/Icon SMI 23; Rich Graessle Icon CGV 24; Scott Grau/Icon SW (2) 25; Rich Gabriels/Icon SW 26. **Cover photo:** Focus on Football

About the Author

Craig Ellenport, a freelance writer who resides in Massapequa, New York, has written several kids books about the National Football League.